Brazilian Girls

Hot Sexy Brazilian Lingerie Girls Models Pictures

By **PHOTO ART LOVER**

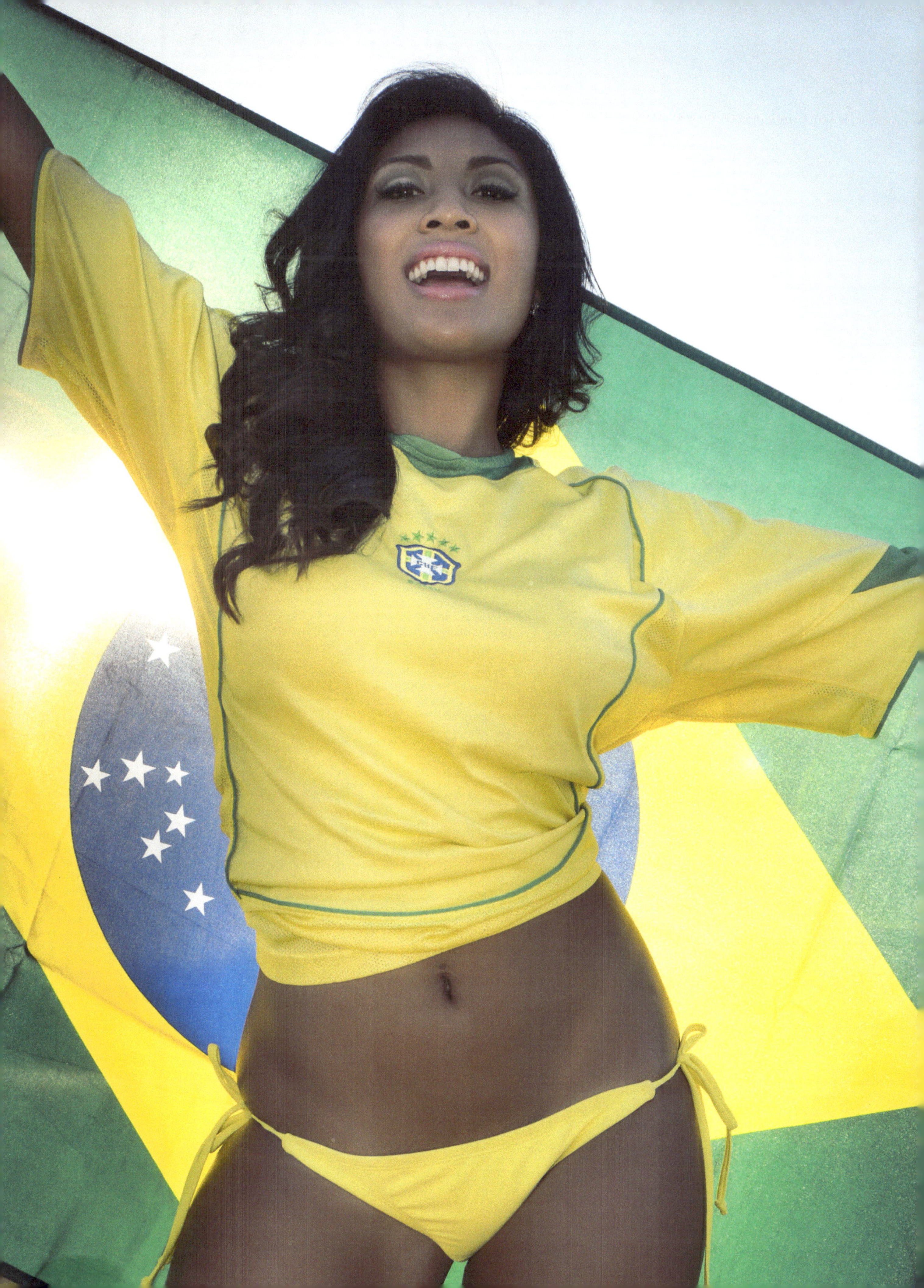

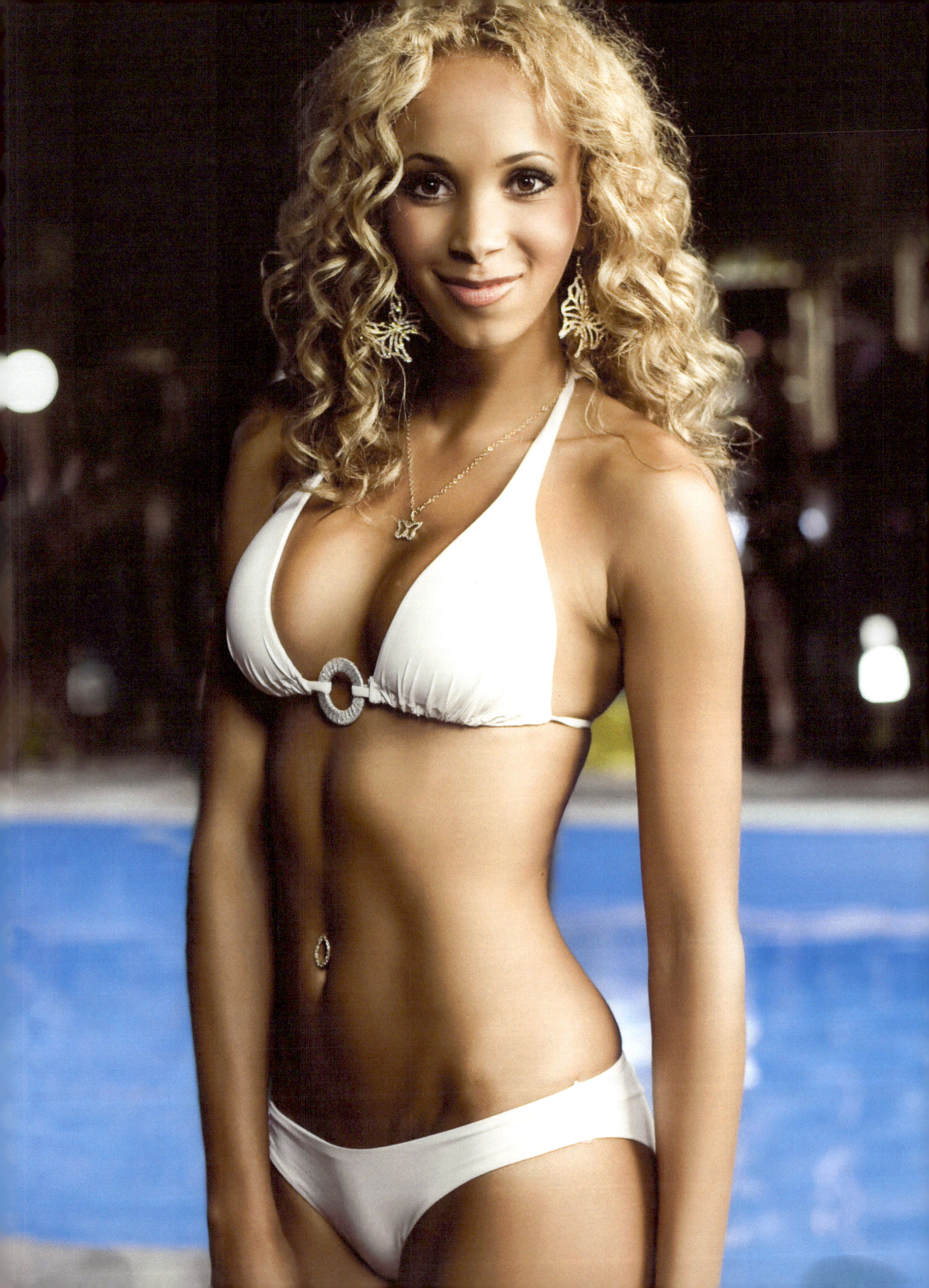

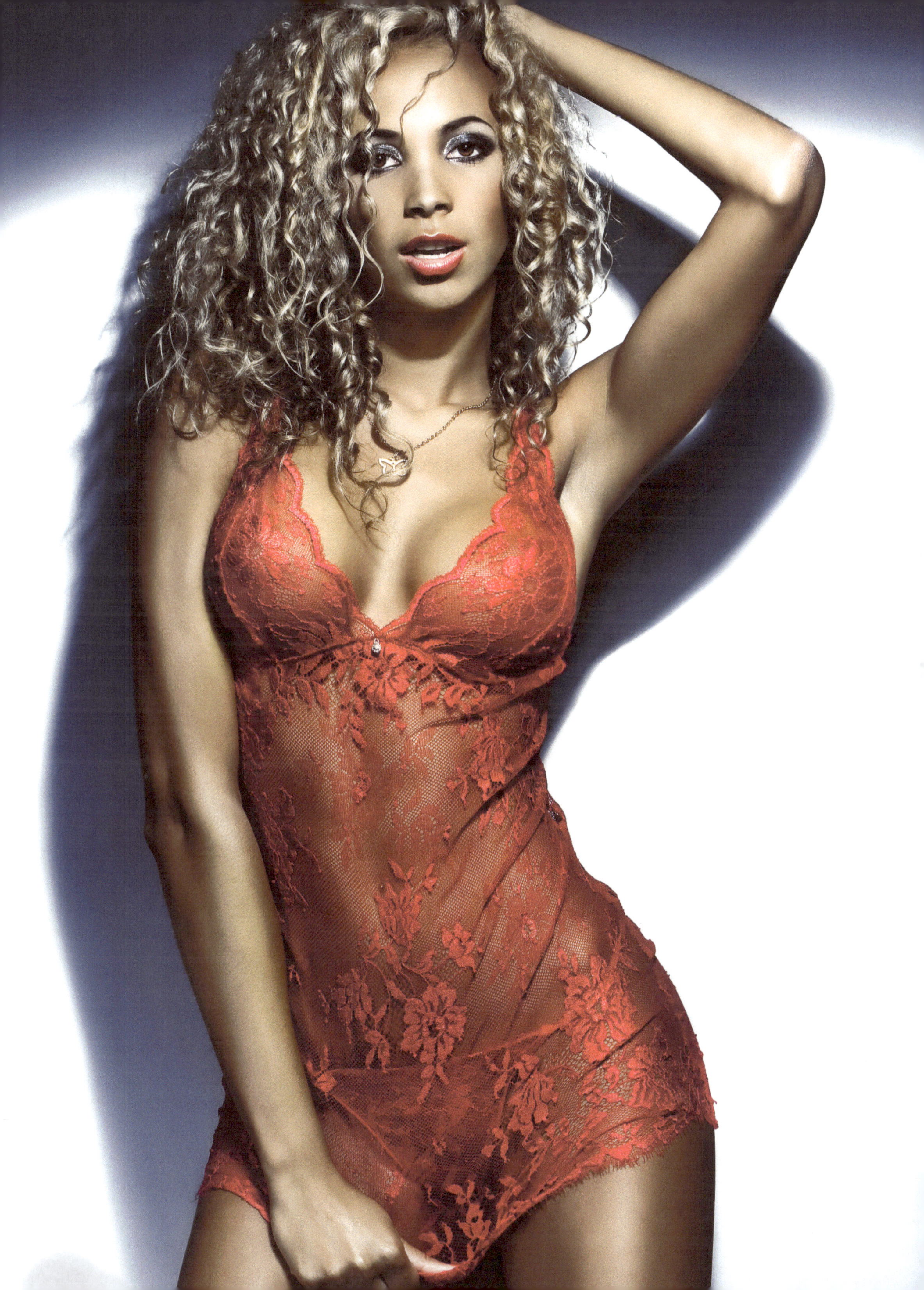

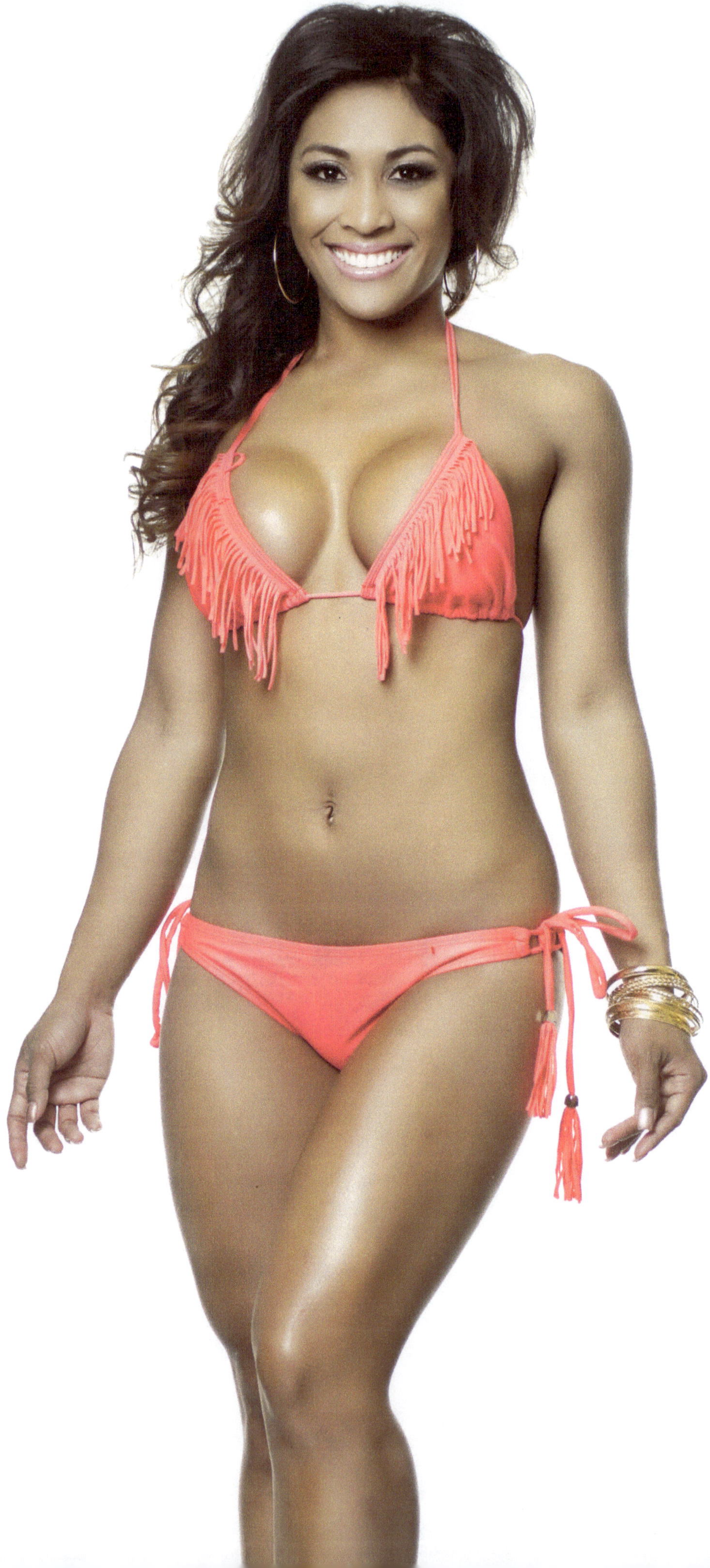

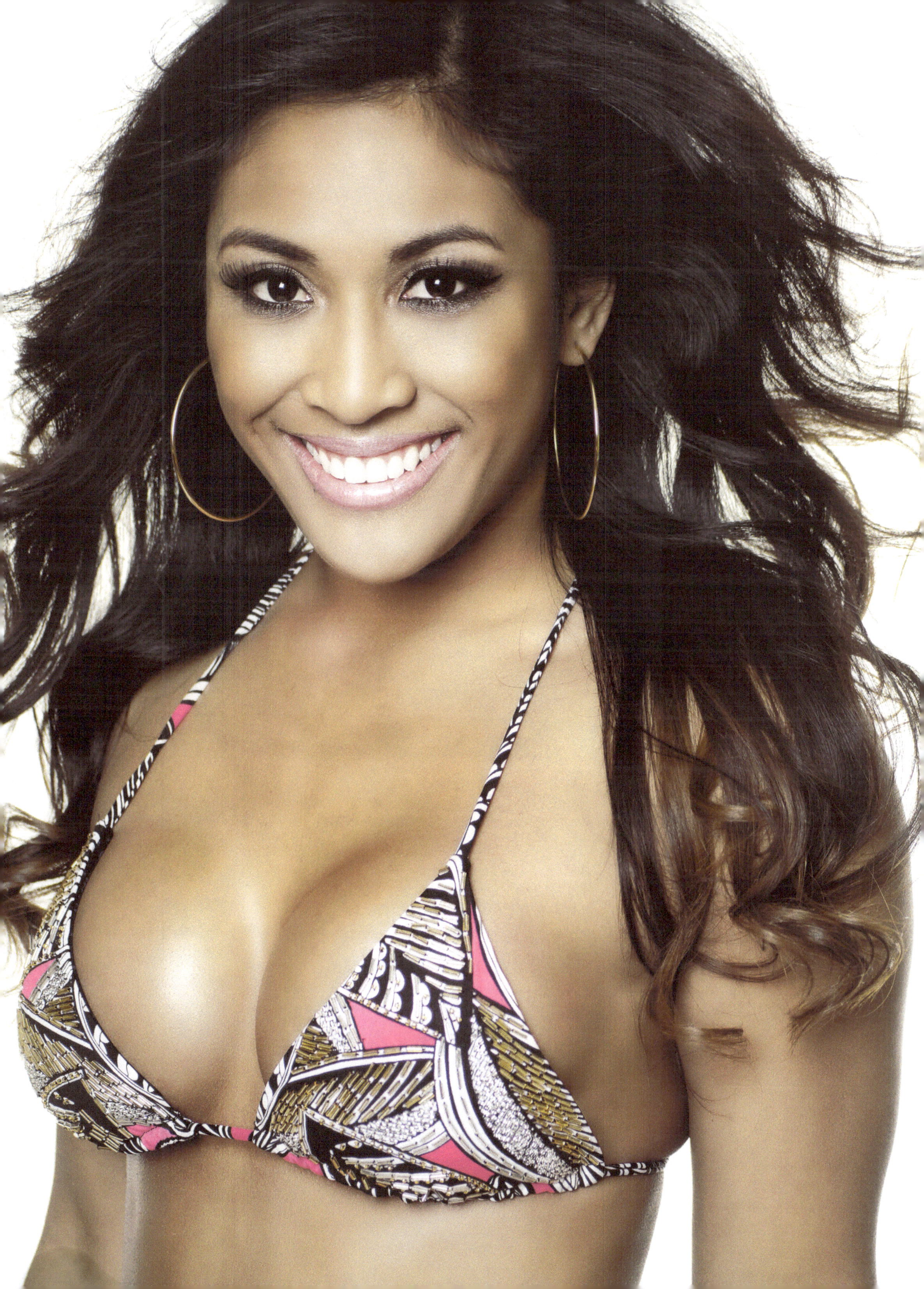

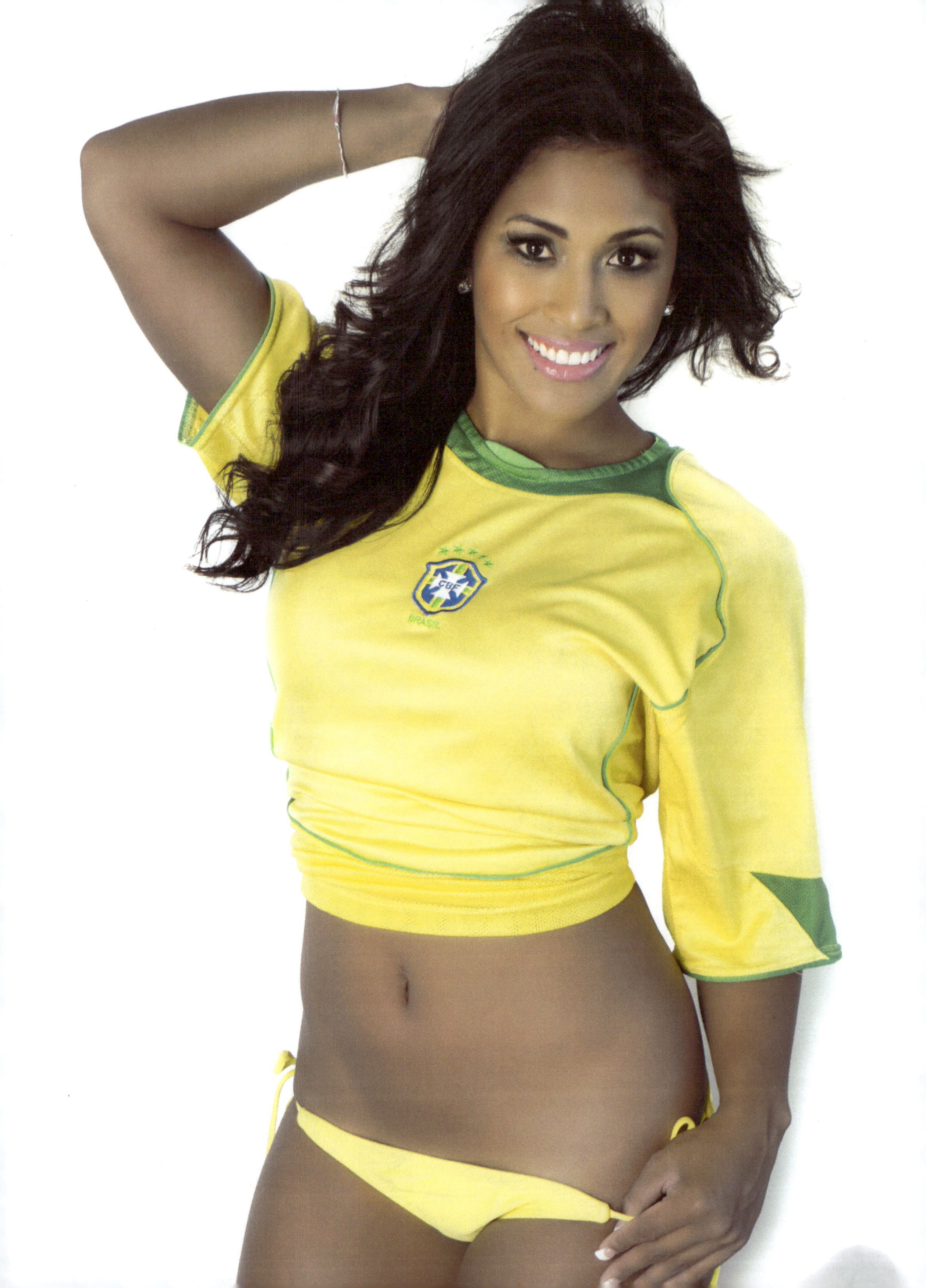
CBF
BRASIL

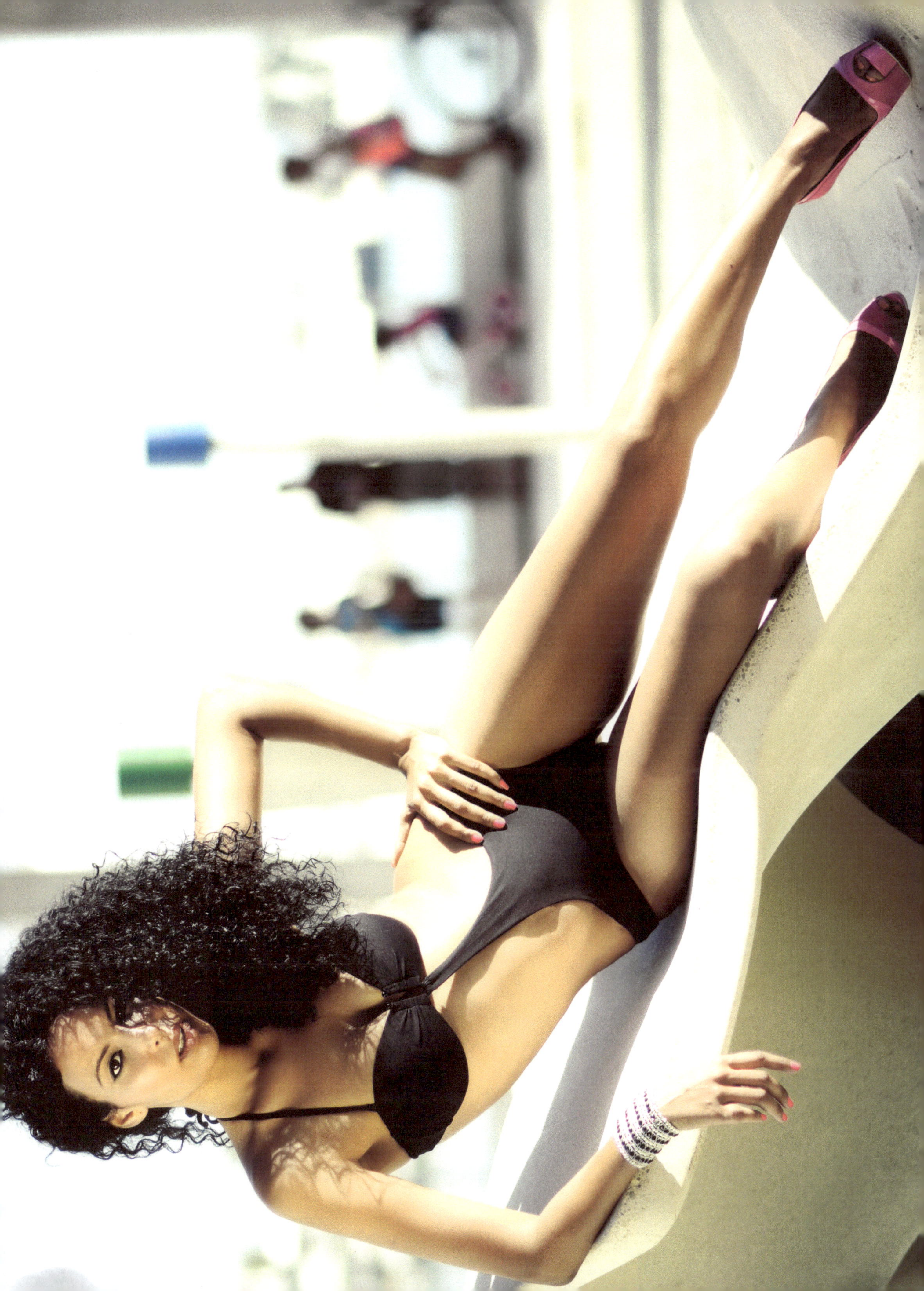

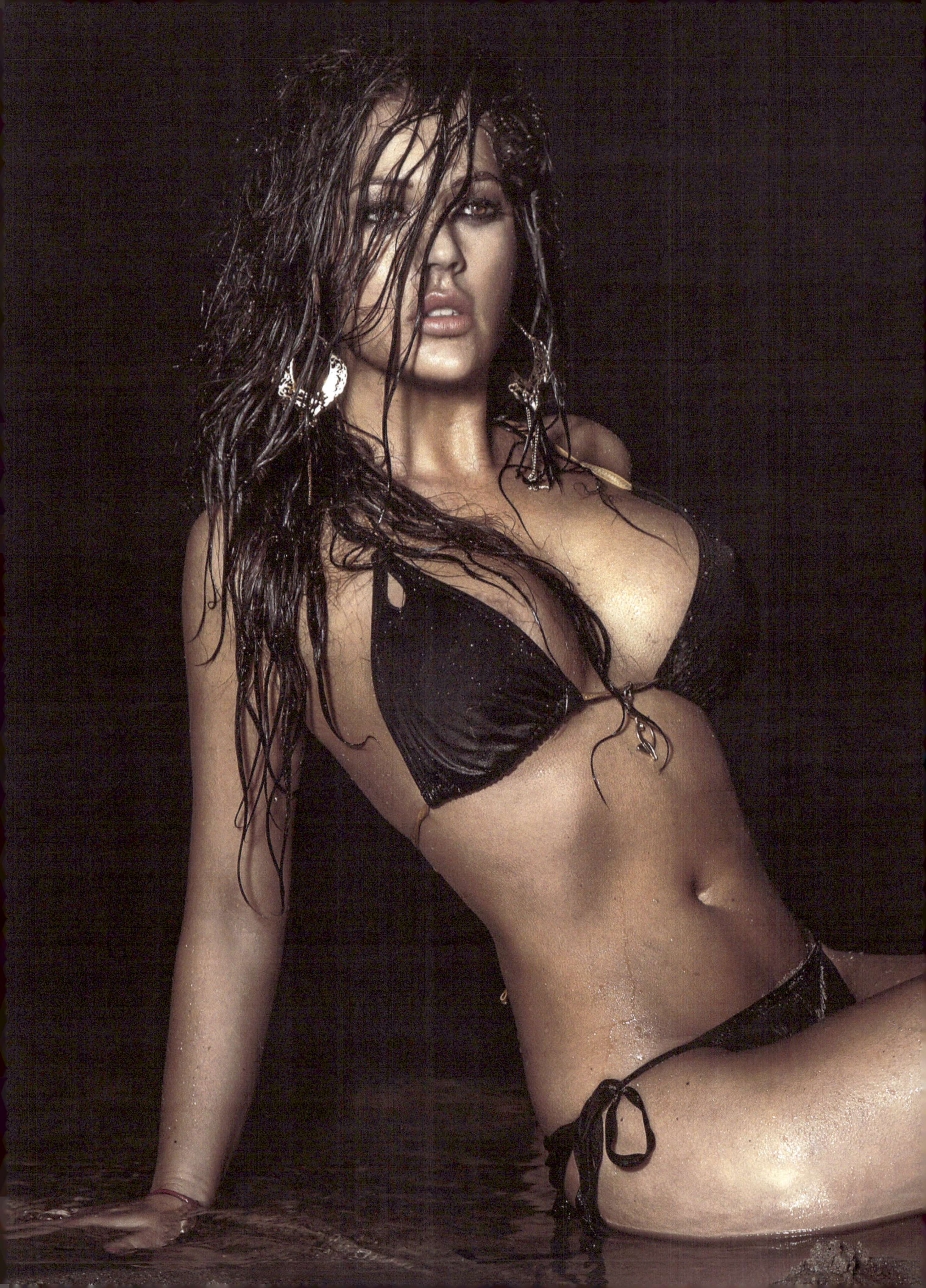

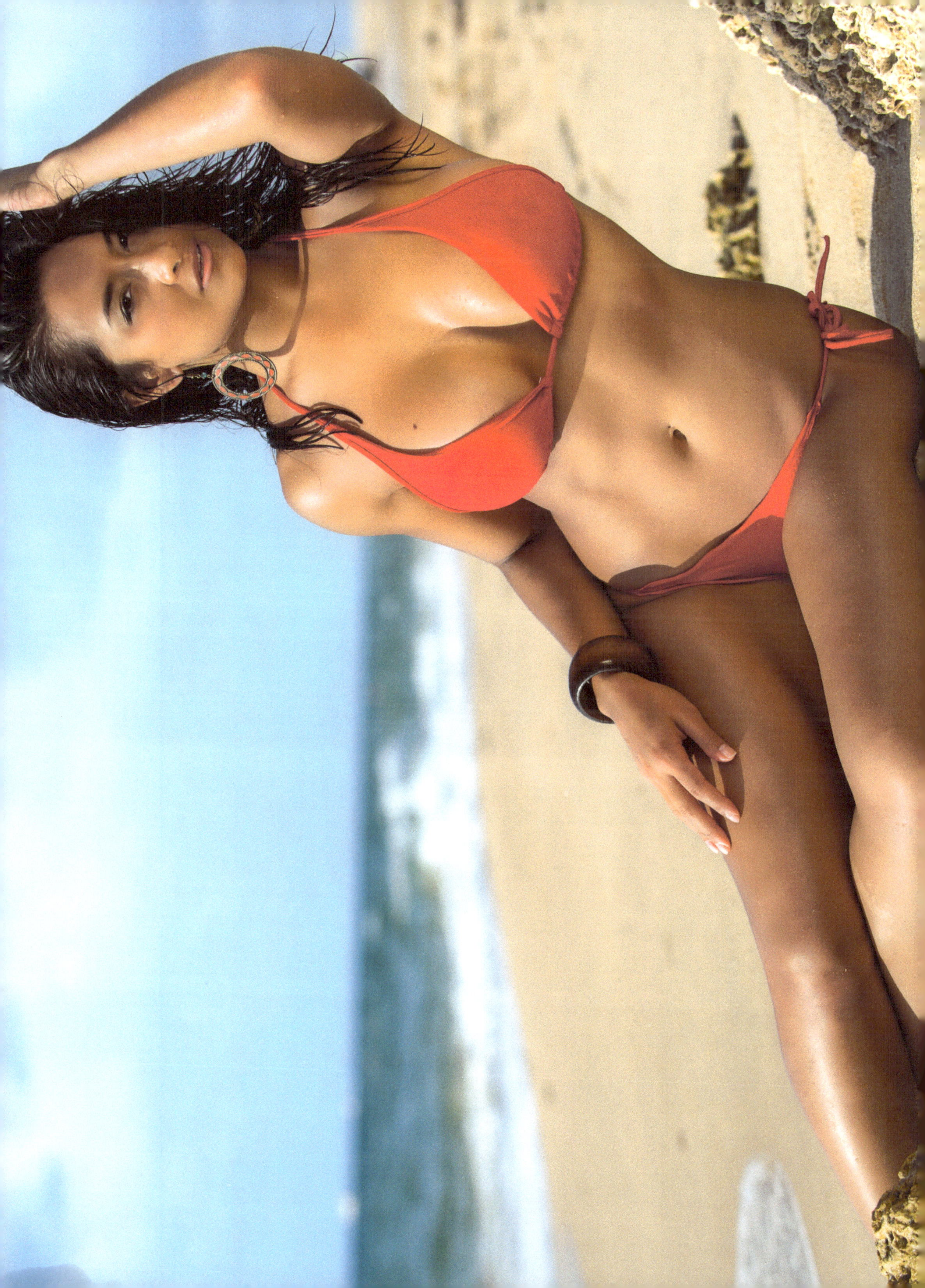

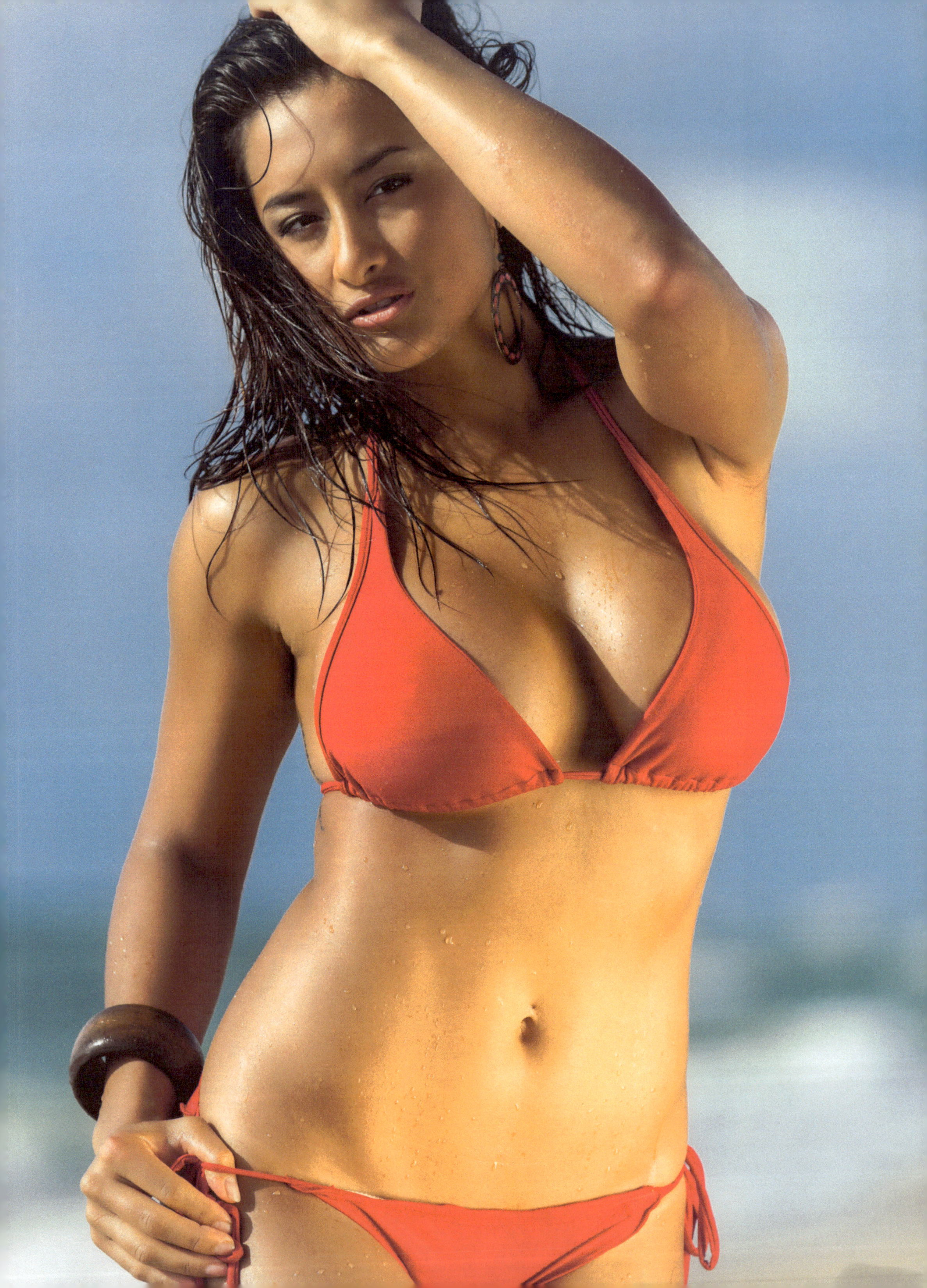

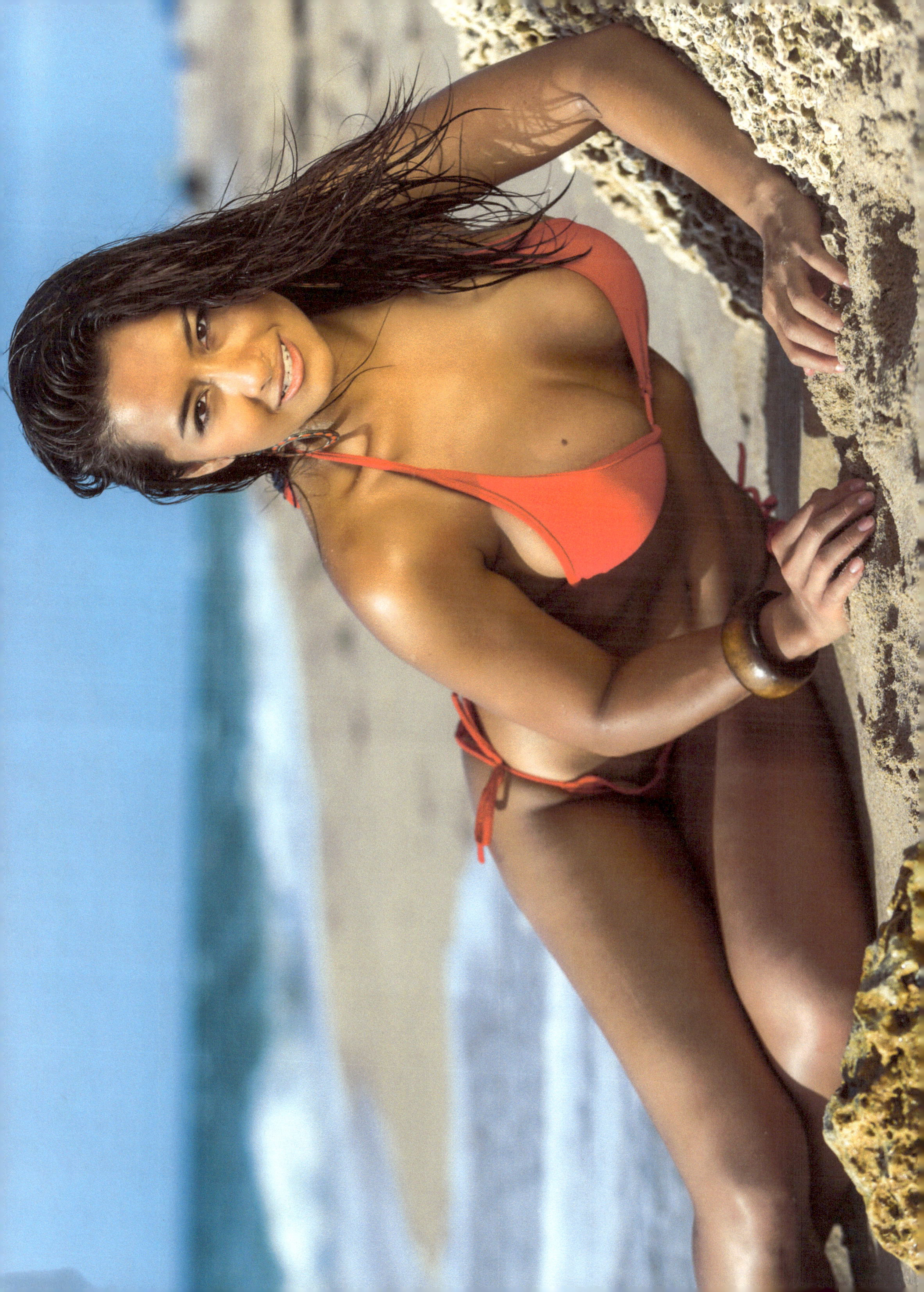

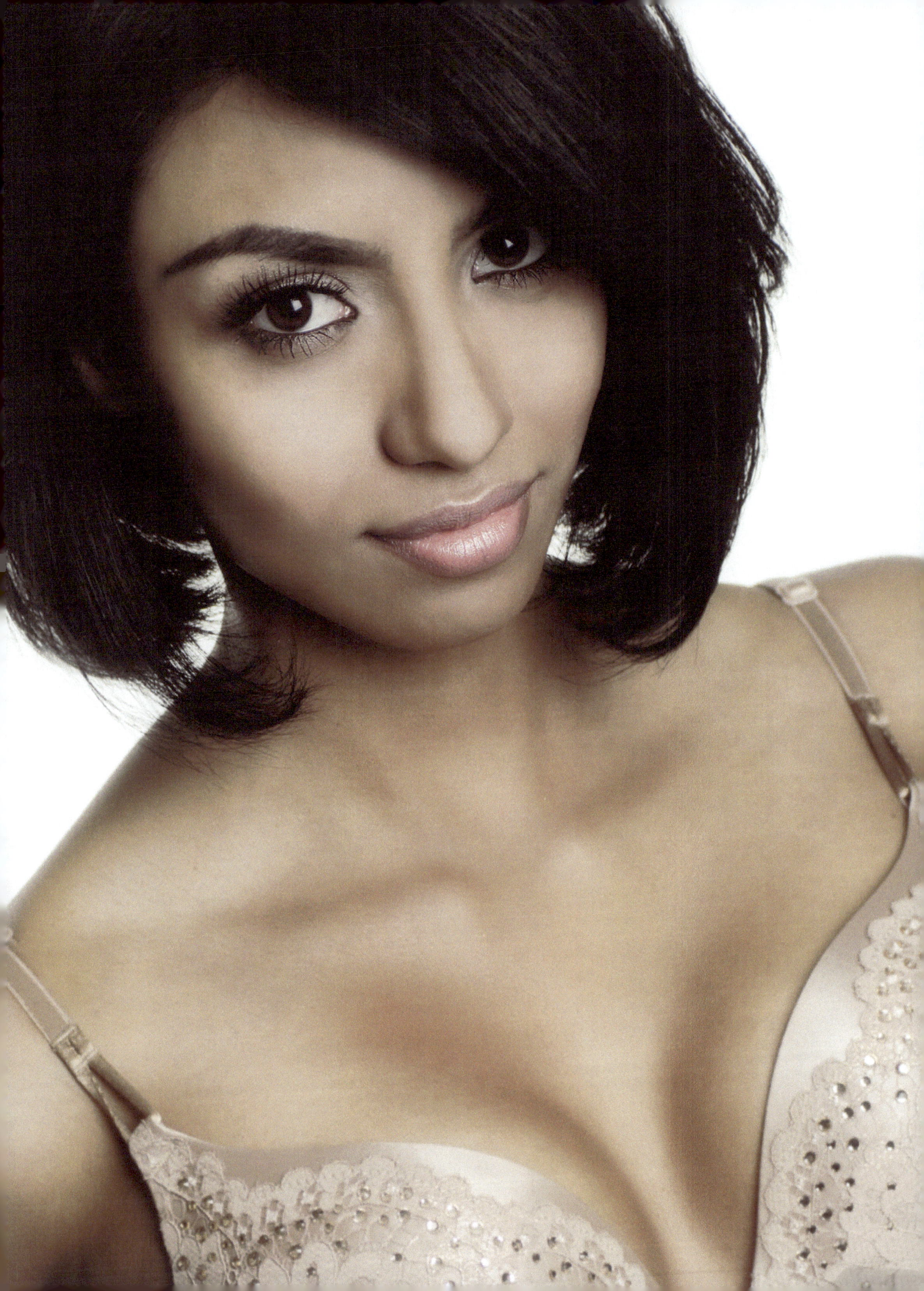

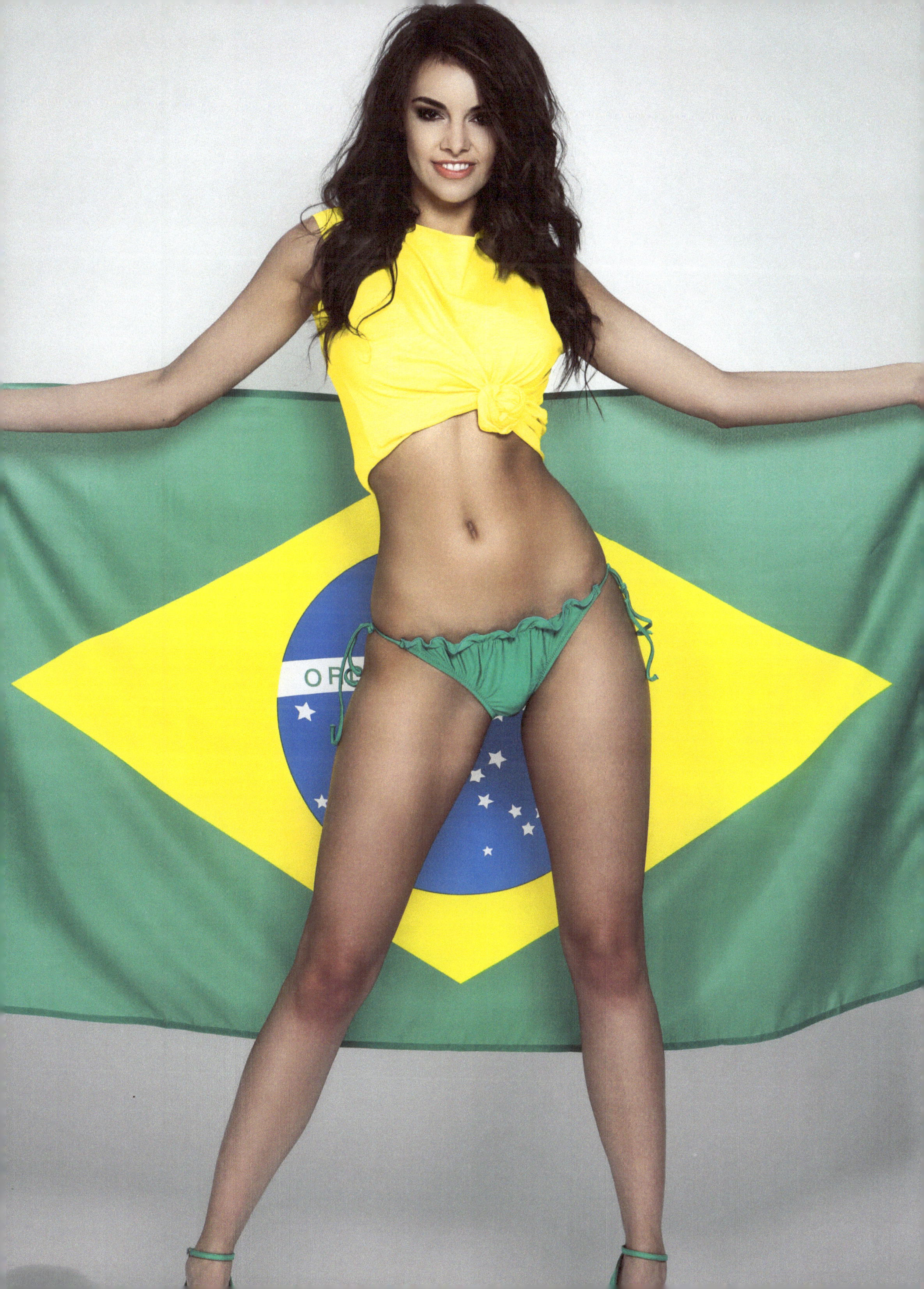

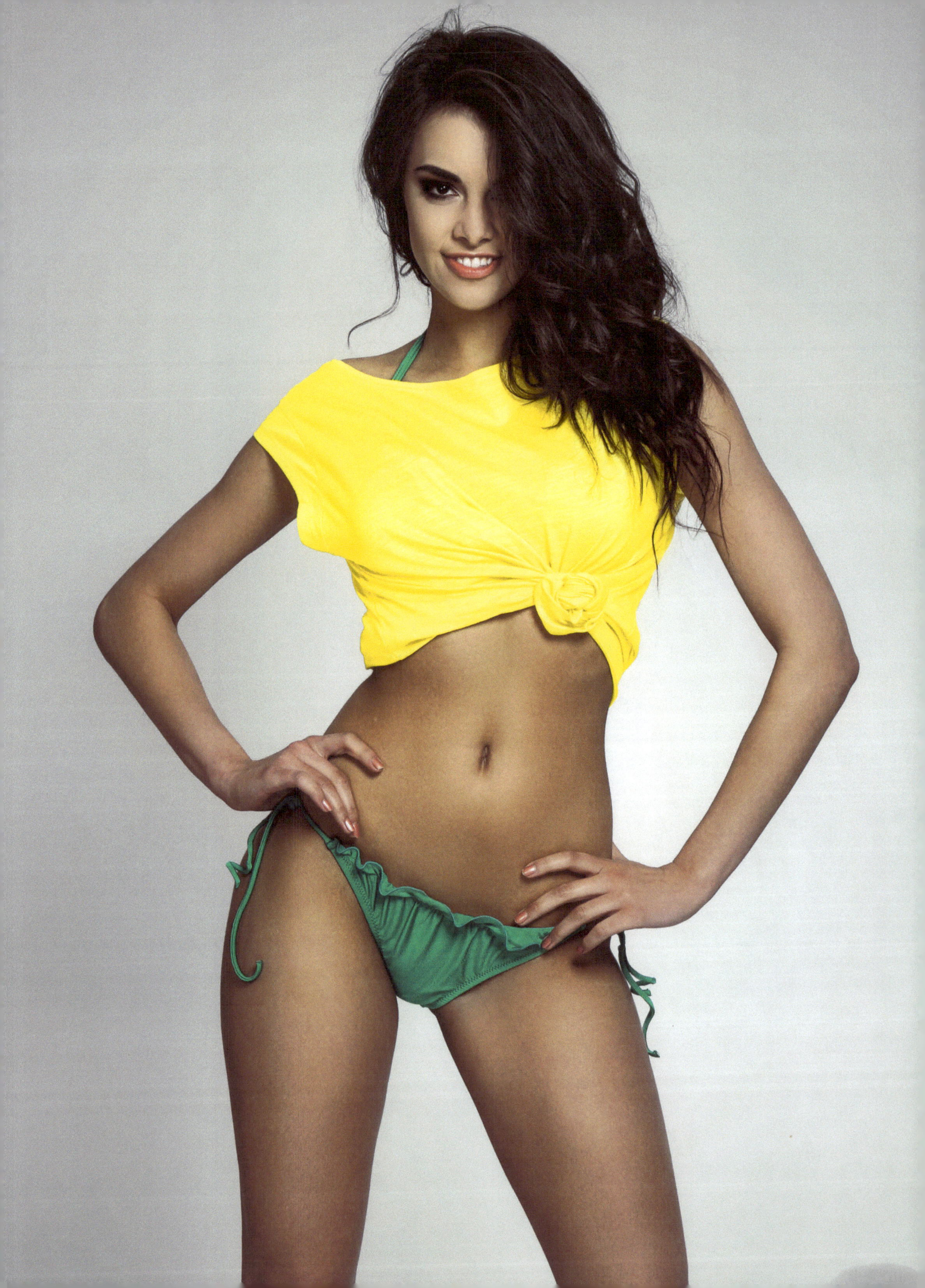

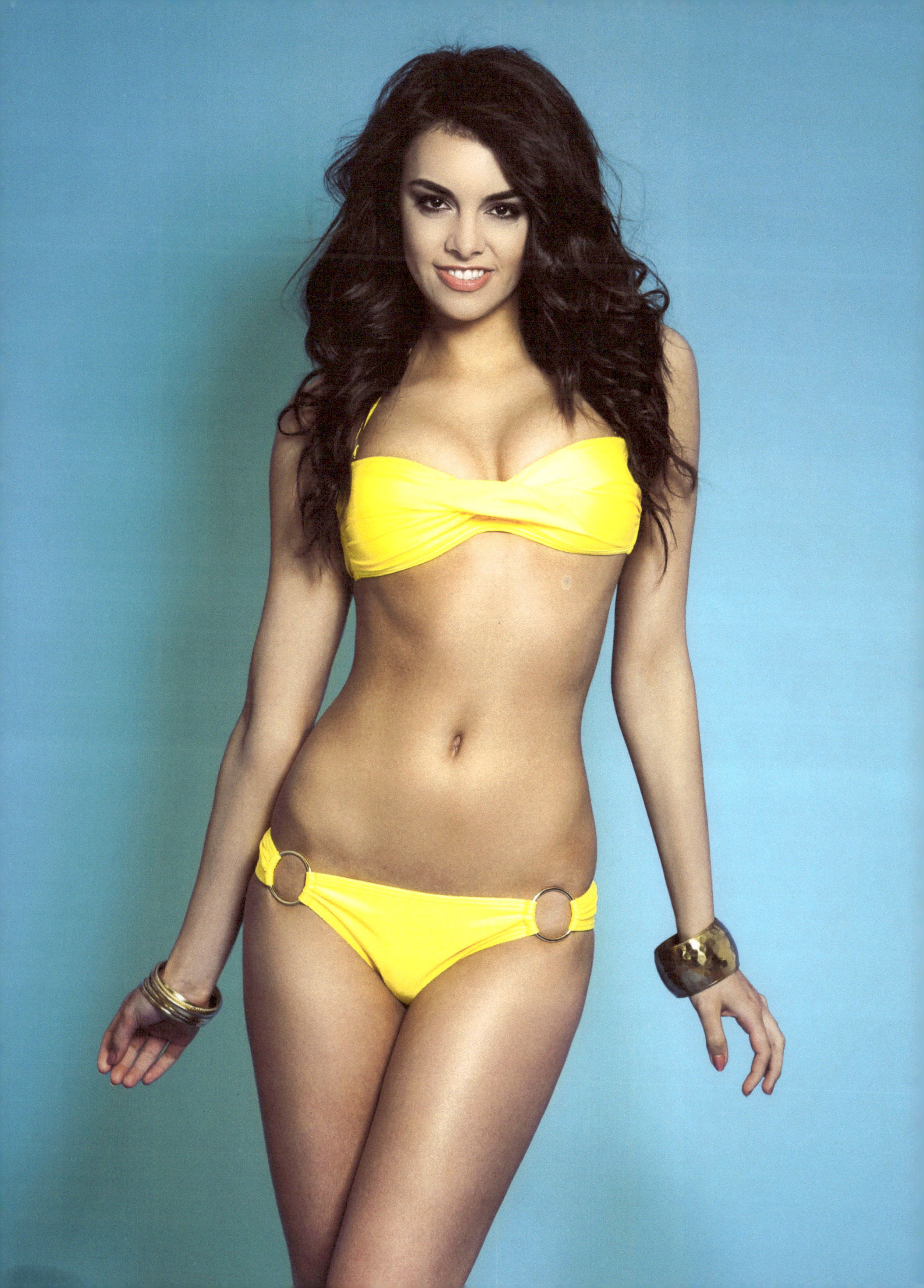

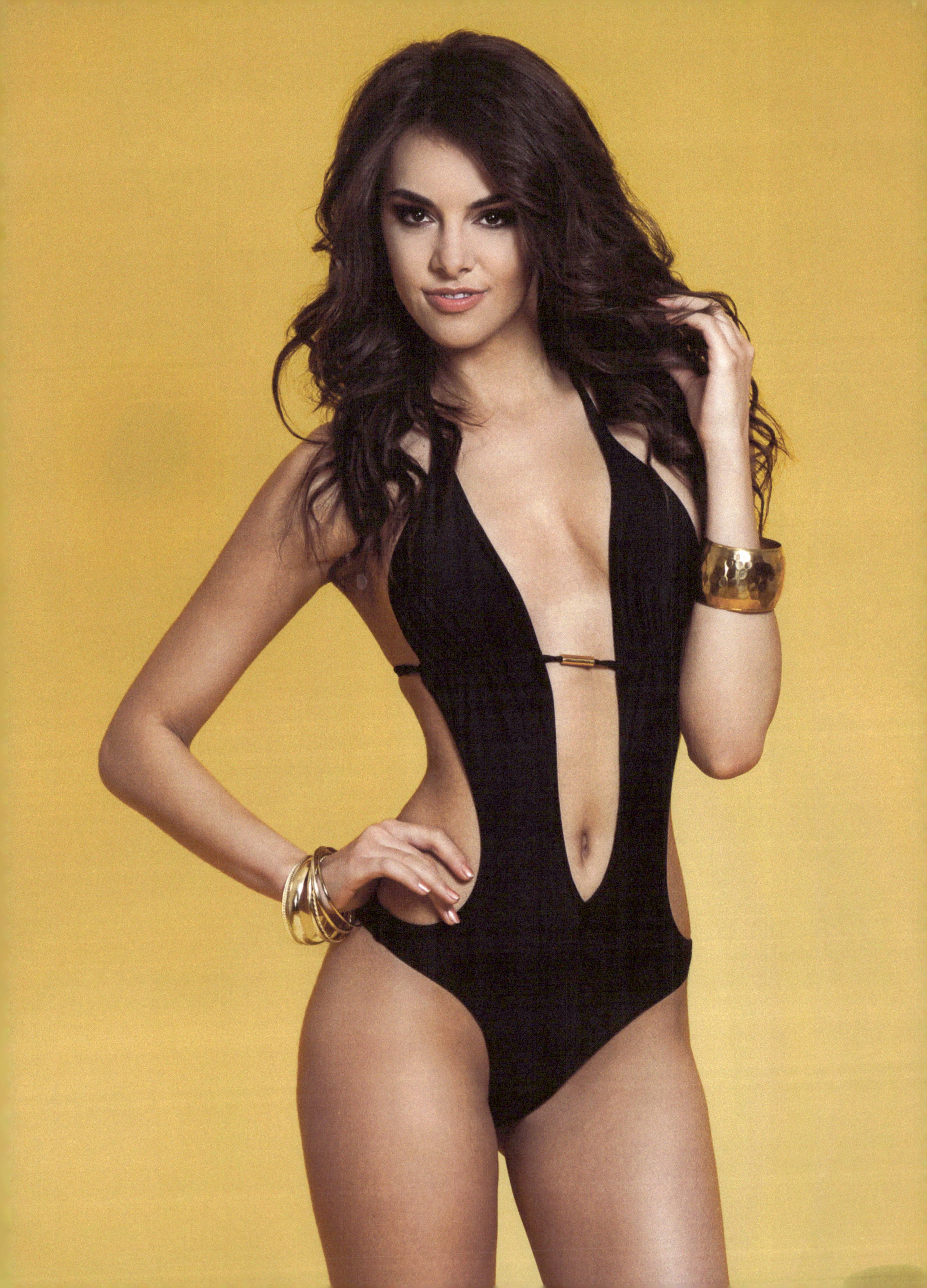

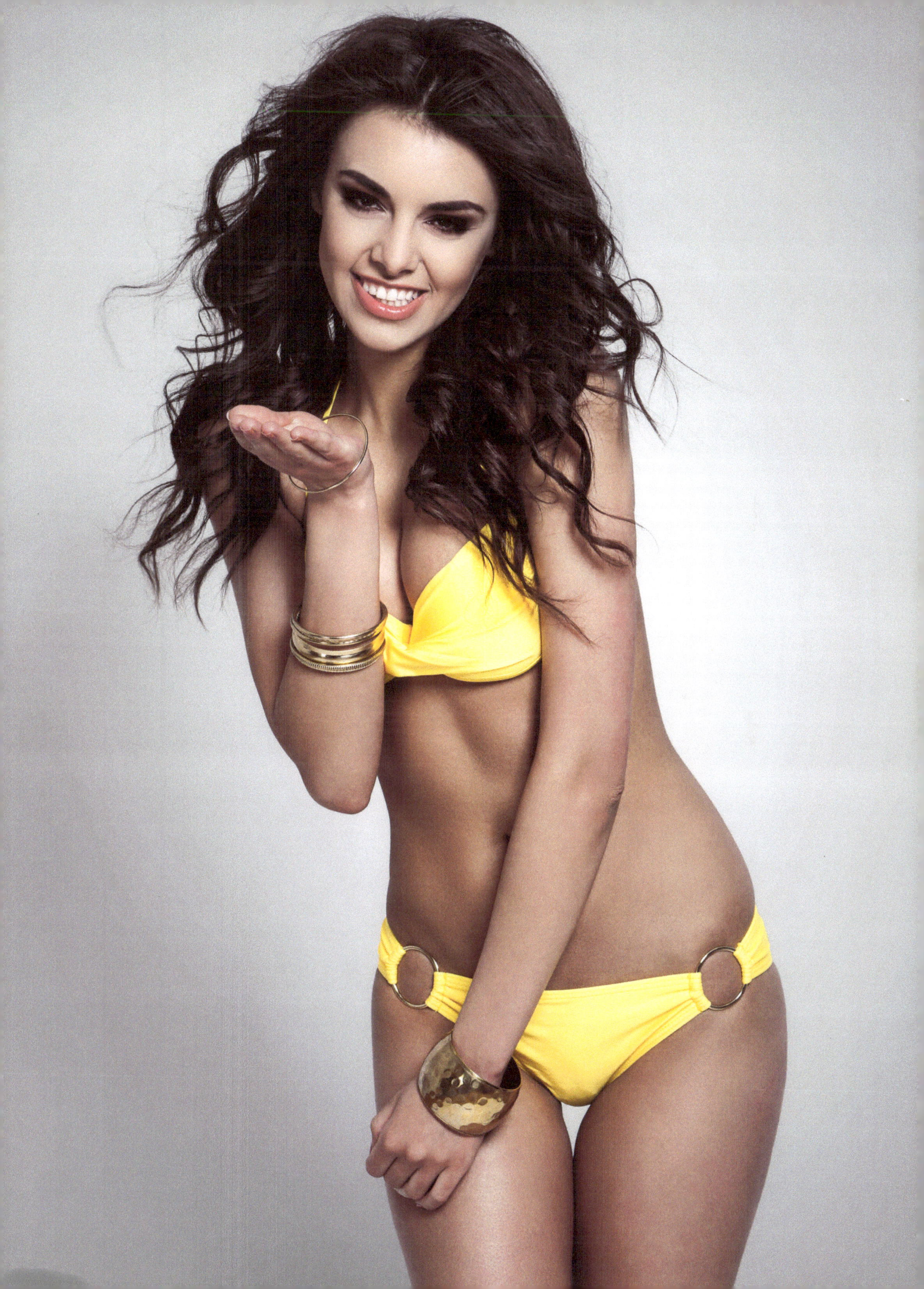

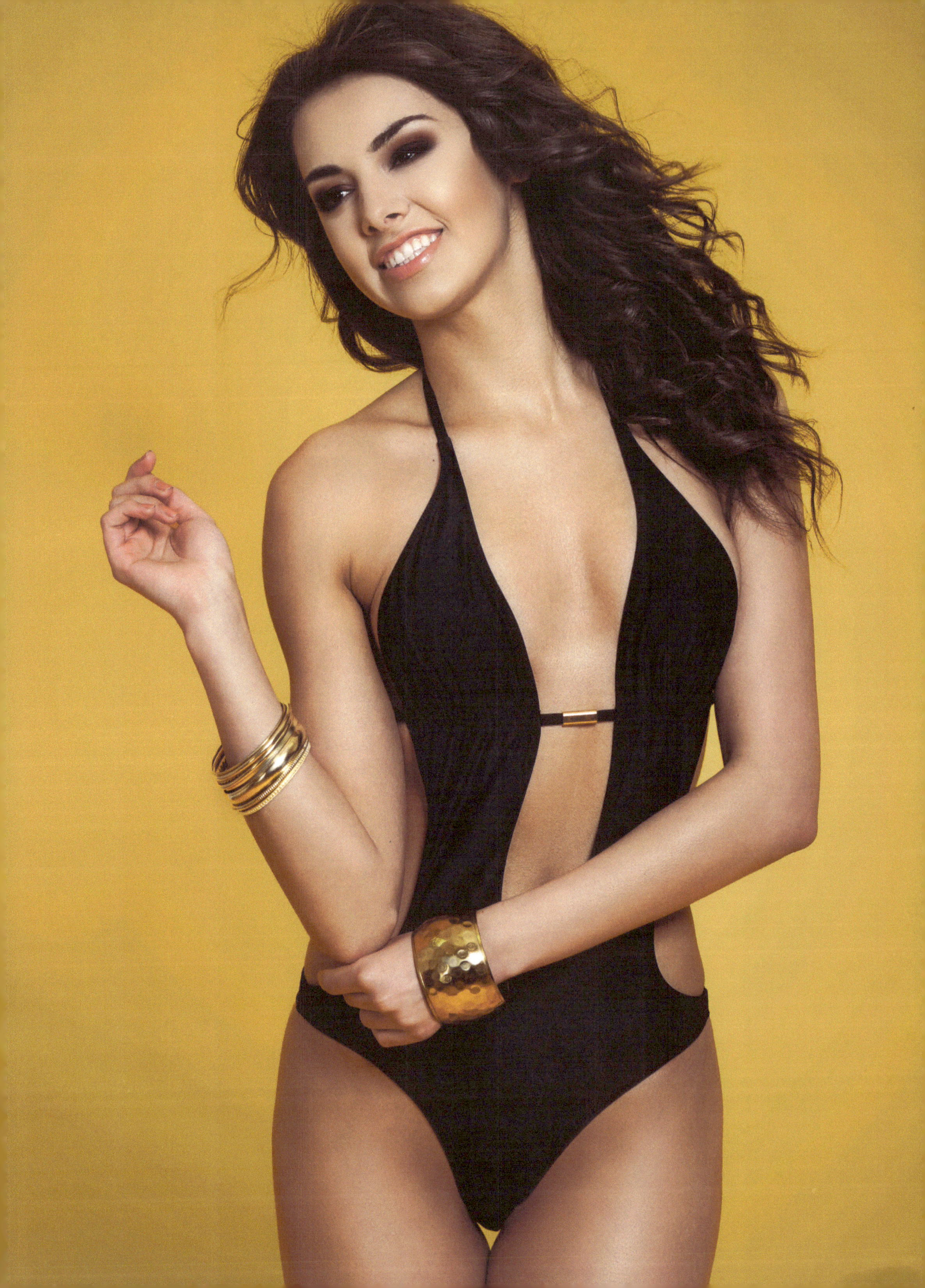

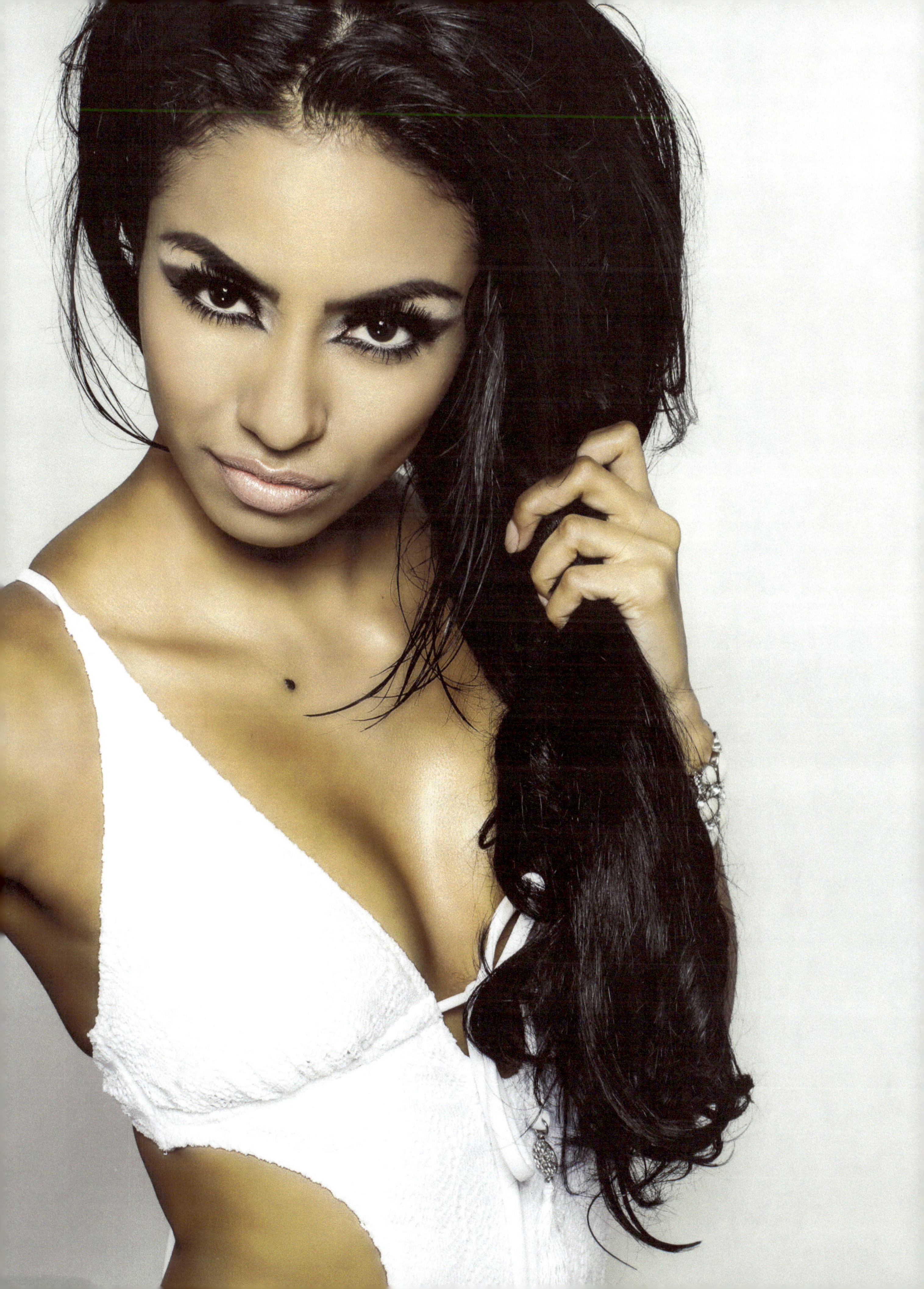

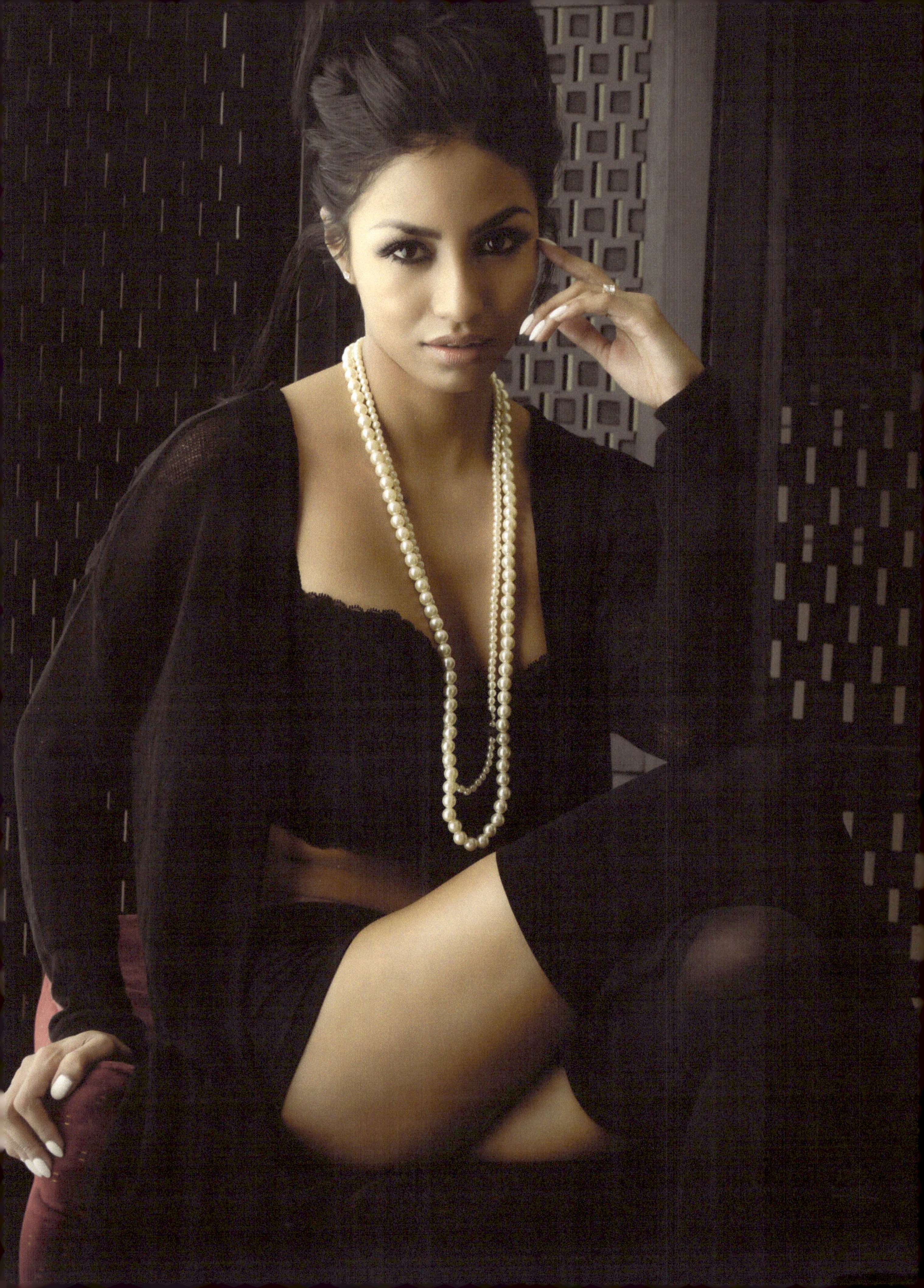

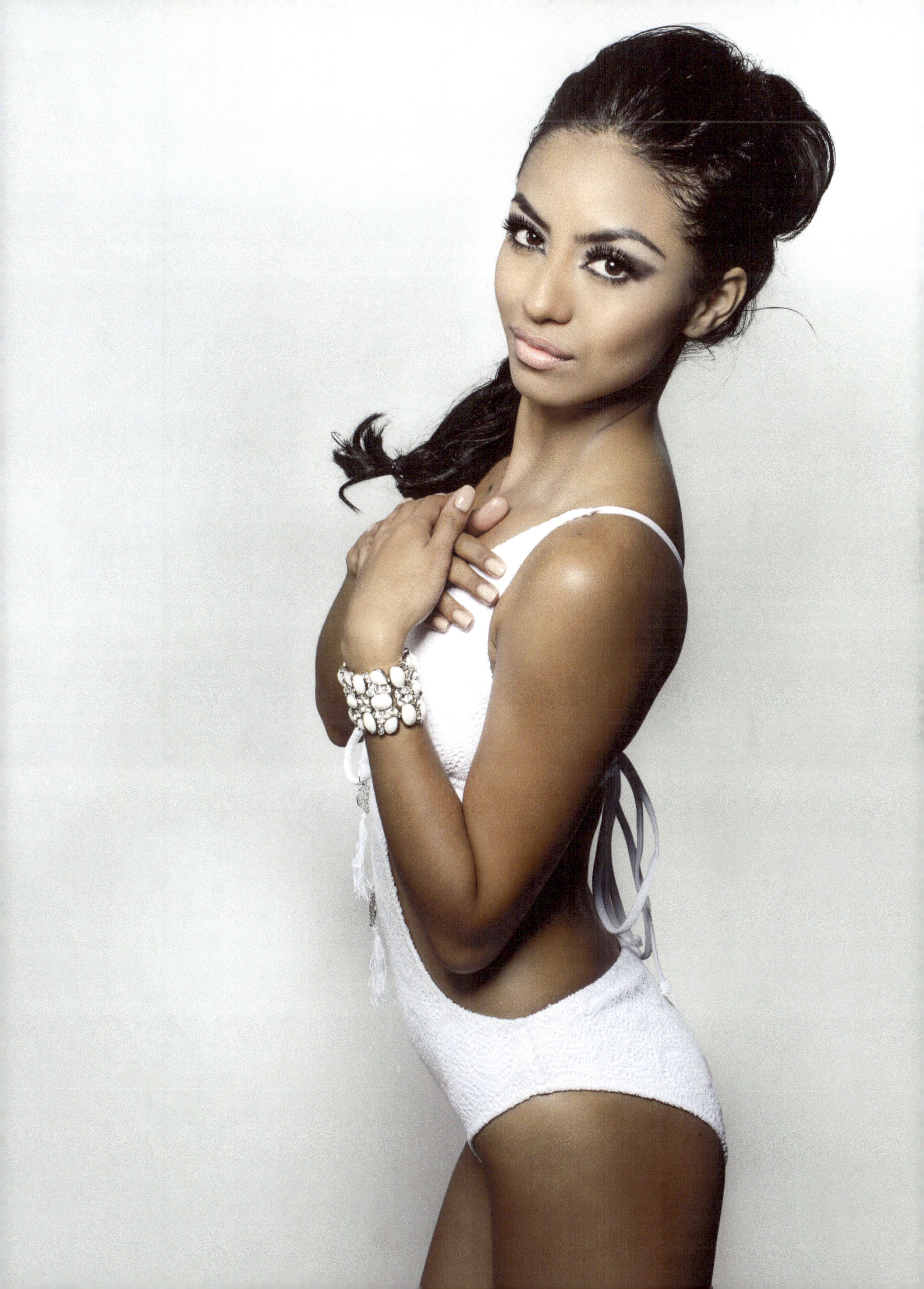

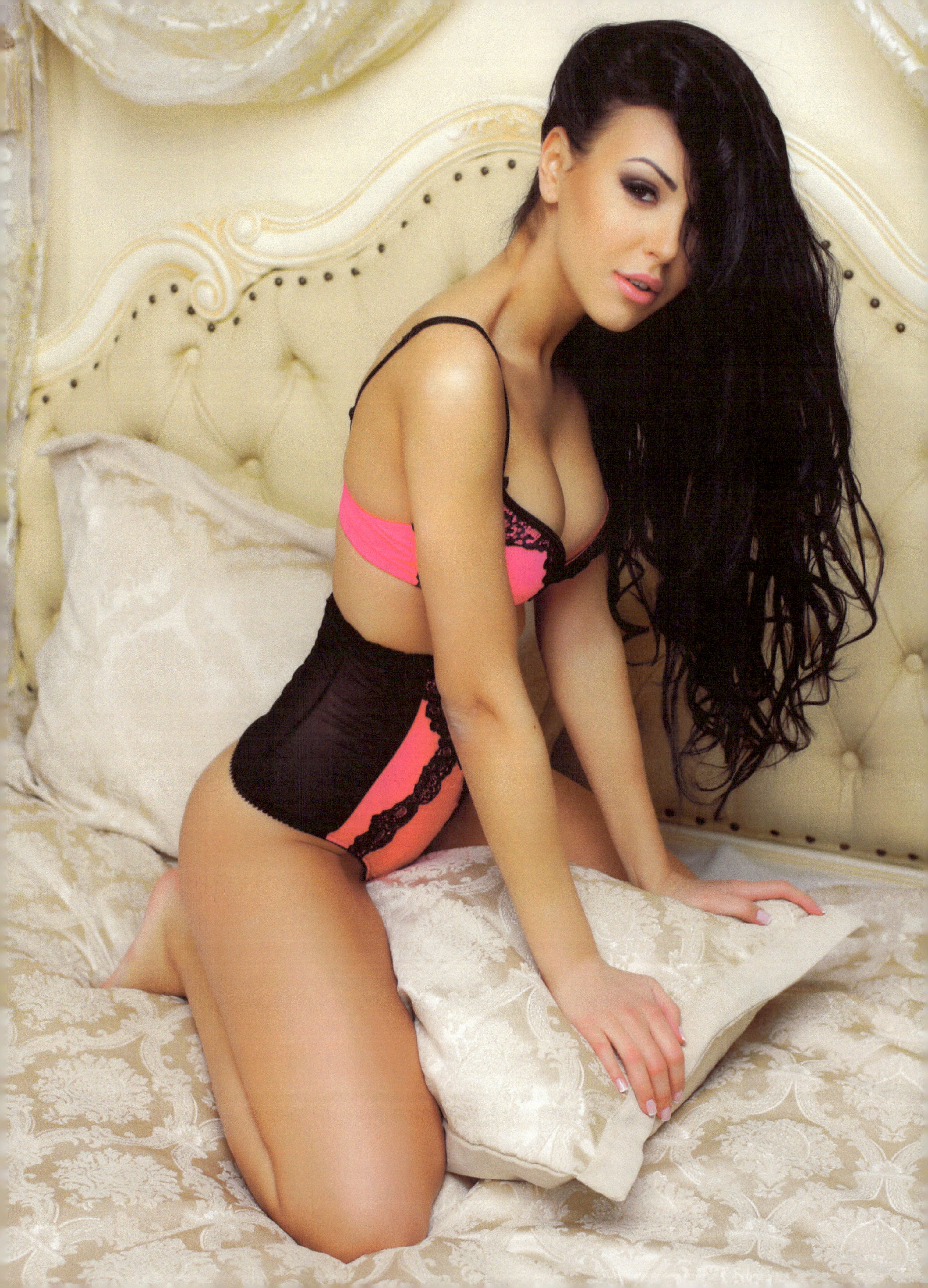

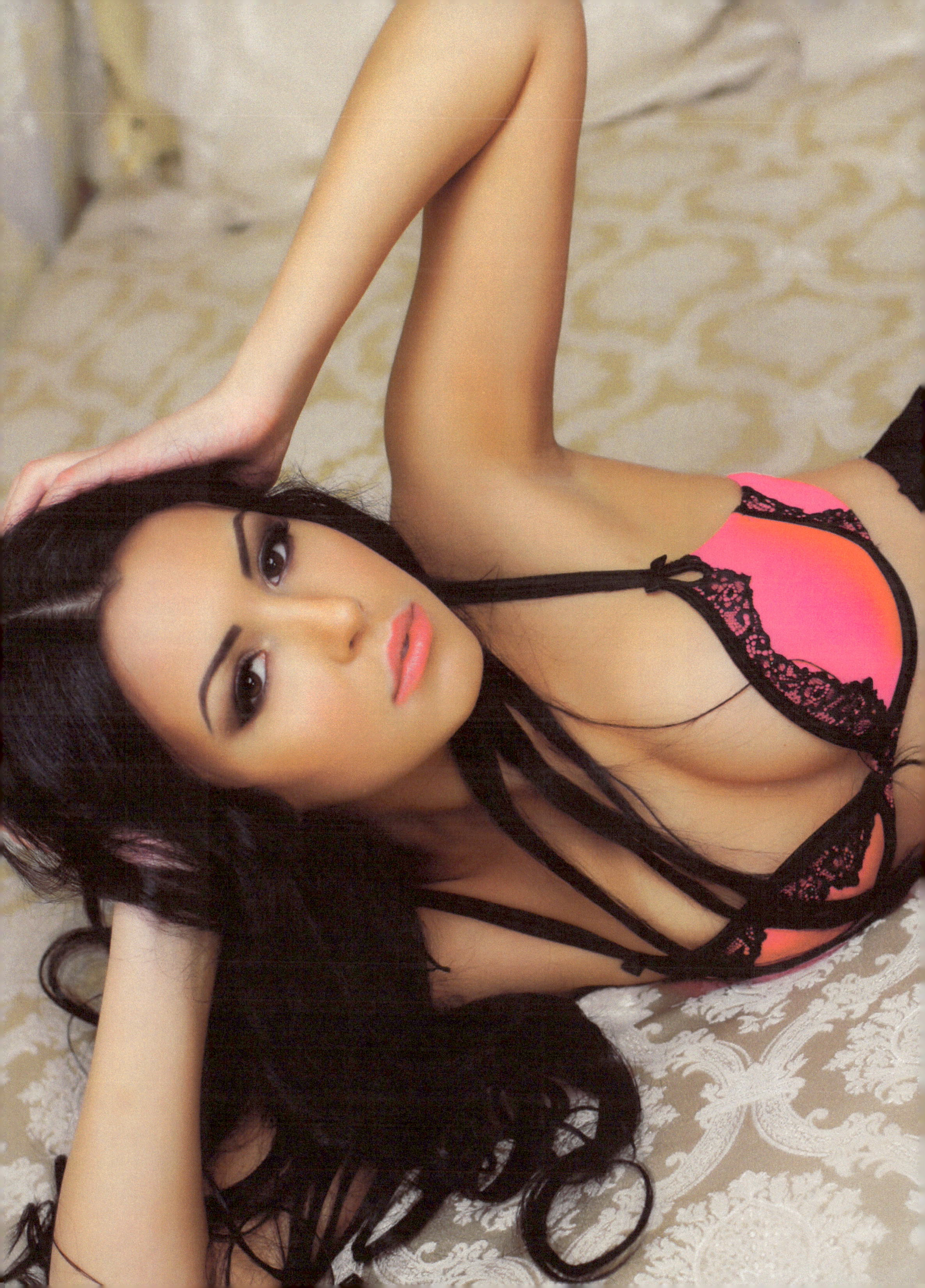

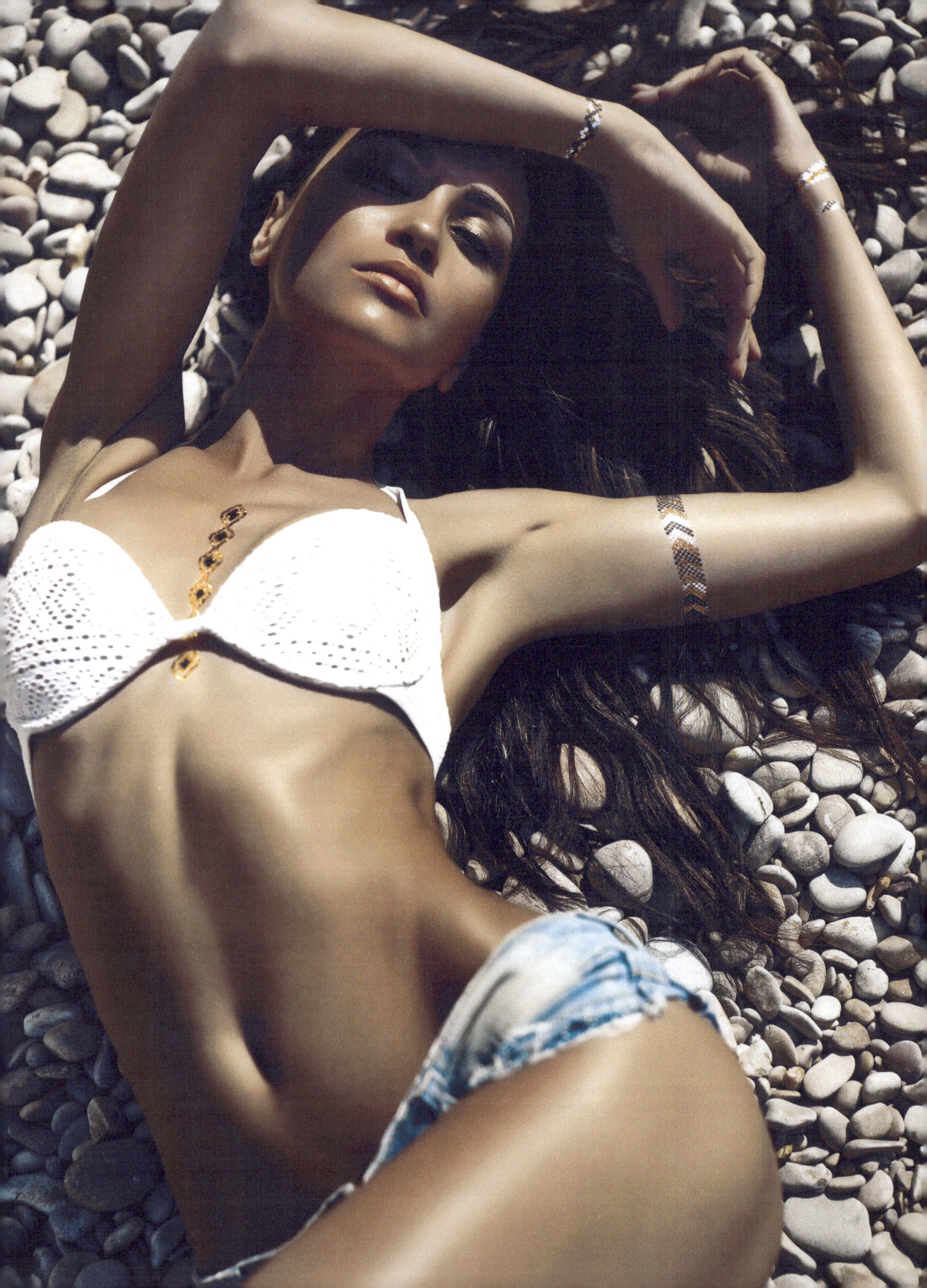

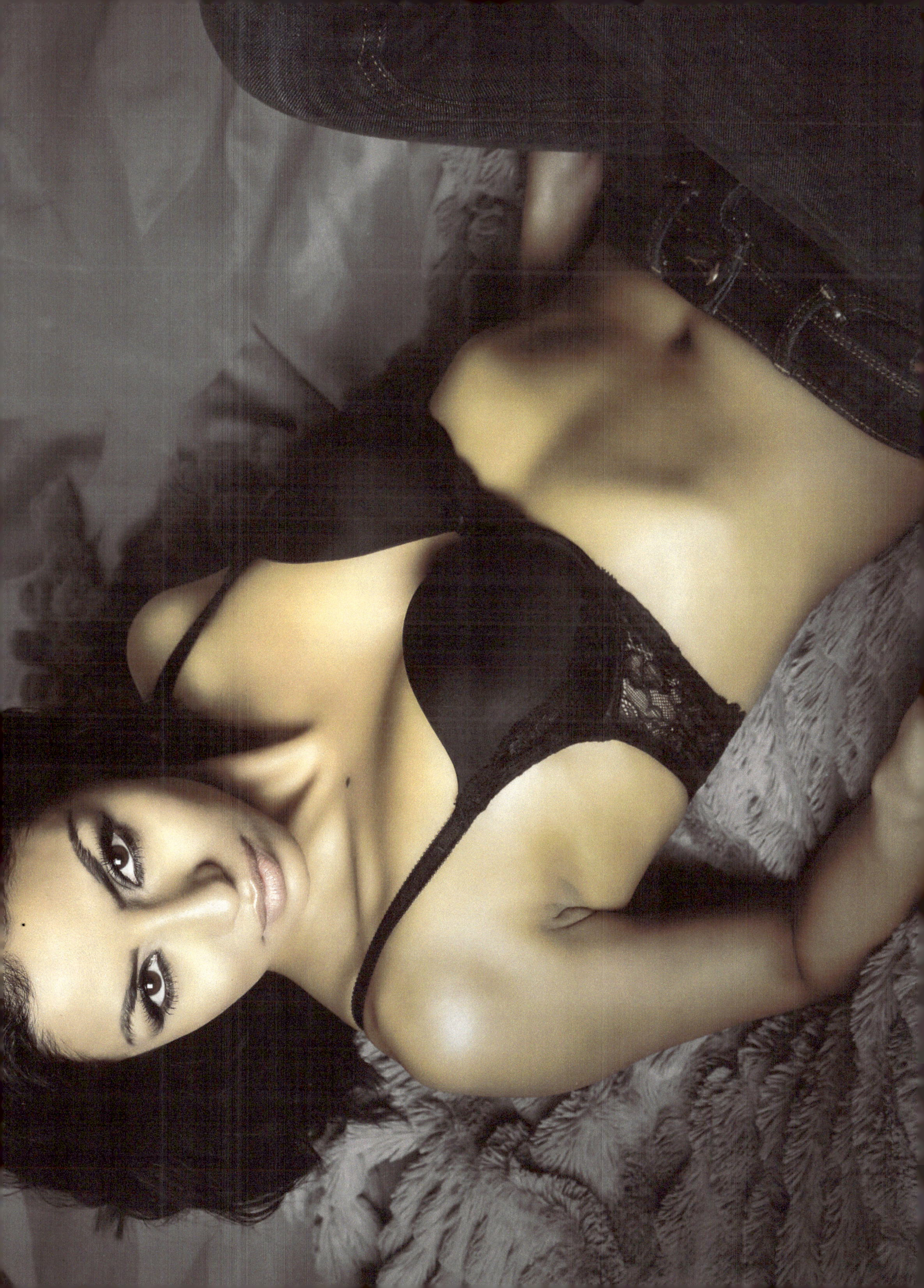

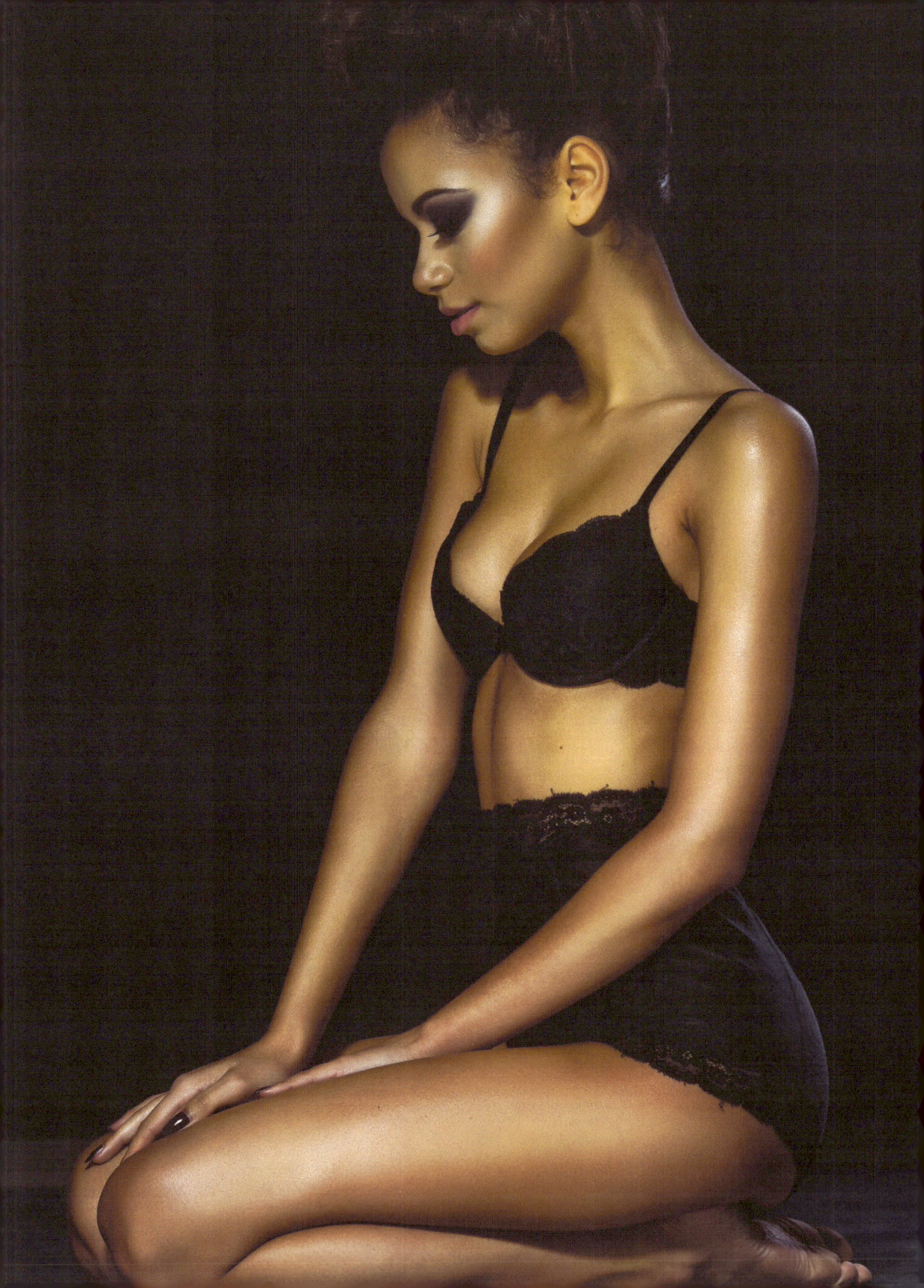

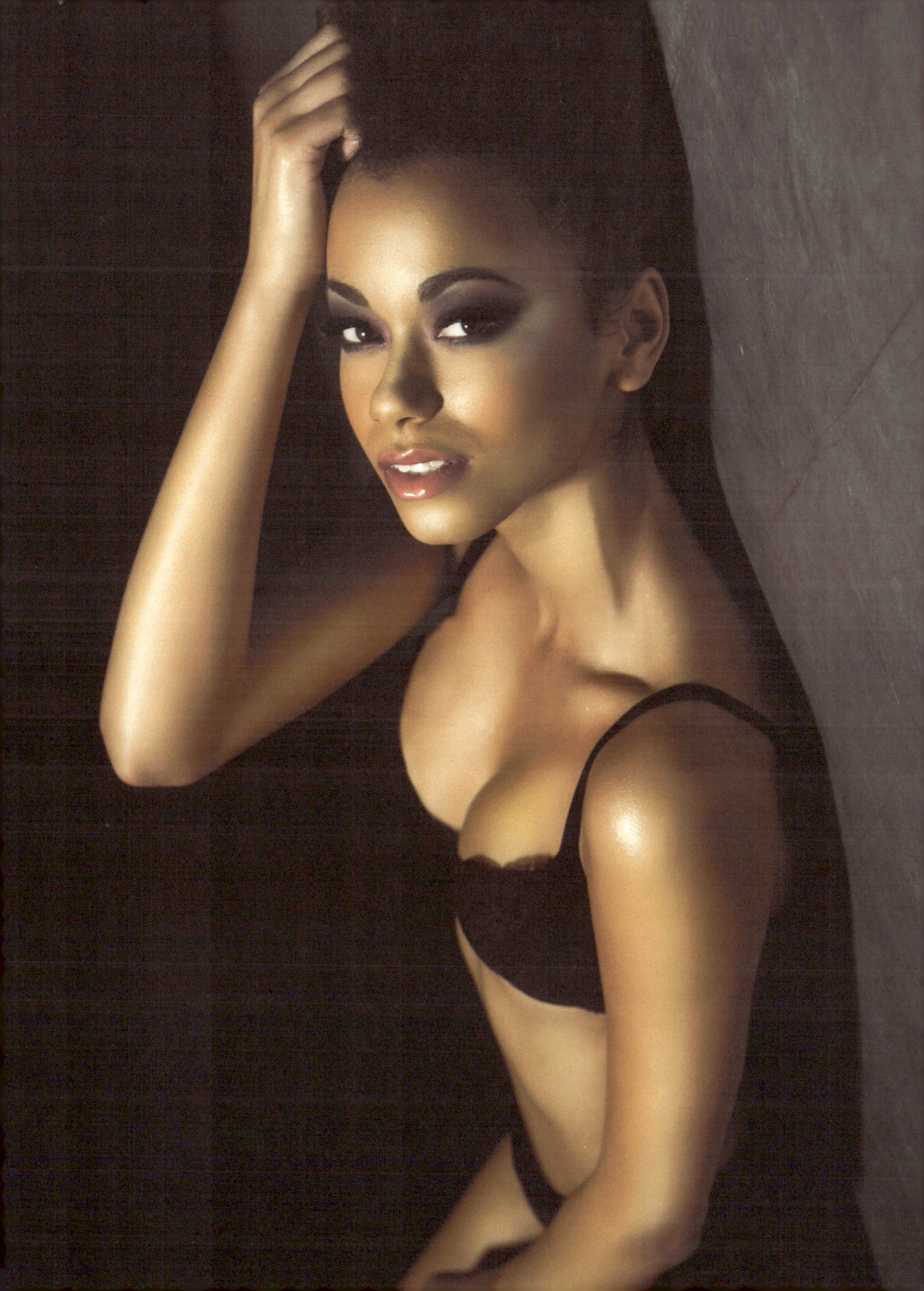

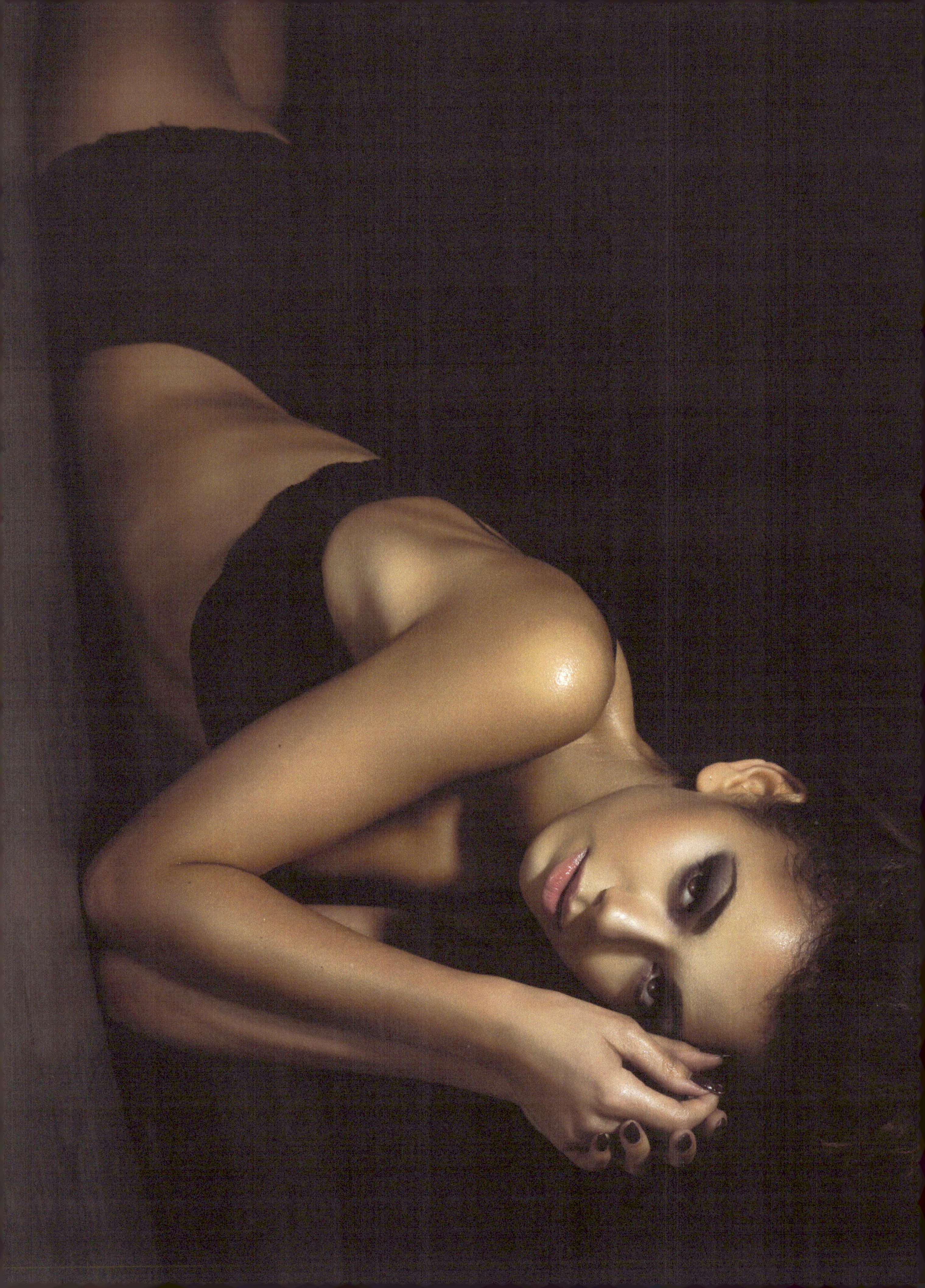

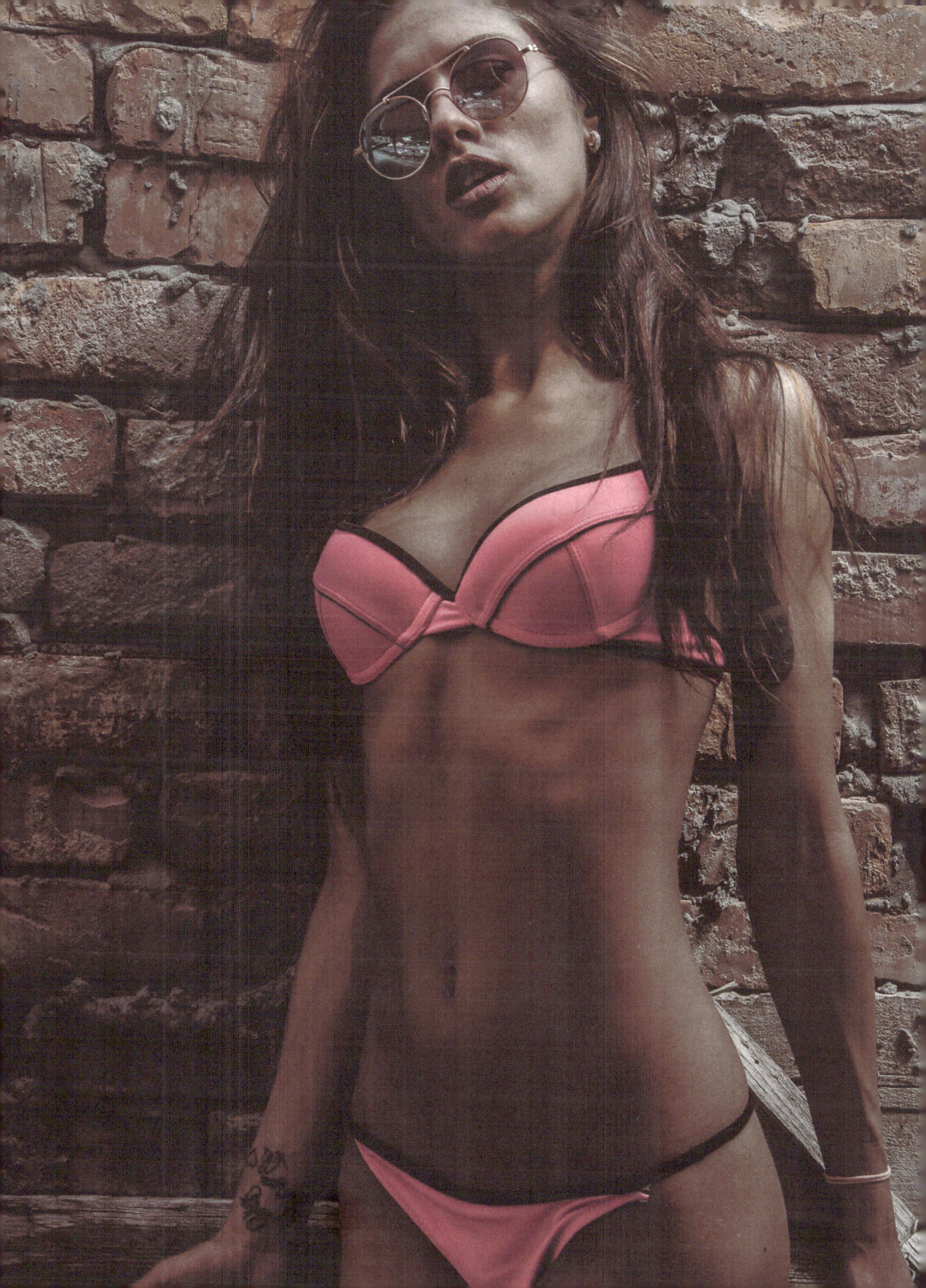

www.ingramcontent.com/pod-product-compliance
Lightning Source LLC
Chambersburg PA
CBHW050418180526
45159CB00005B/2317